AF148249

The
ROMANS
Invasion and Empire

by Ruth Owen

Consultant: Dr. Rebecca Redfern
The Museum of London

Ruby Tuesday Books

Map of the Roman Empire

N E S W

Caspian Sea

Black Sea

Red Sea

MODERN-DAY TURKEY

EGYPT

GREECE

Mediterranean Sea

MODERN-DAY ITALY
○ Rome

Europe

Africa

MODERN-DAY SPAIN

GAUL (Modern-day France)

North Sea

Hadrian's Wall

BRITANNIA
◎ Londinium

ATLANTIC OCEAN

The Roman Empire at the beginning of the 2nd century AD

Contents

The Invasion of Britannia

Almost 2000 years ago, in the summer of AD 43, a vast army of Roman soldiers assembled on the beaches of Gaul. This was an invasion force and it had one objective — to conquer Britannia!

Under Attack!

Under the command of the Roman General Aulus Plautius, hundreds of ships carrying about 40,000 soldiers crossed the Channel and landed in England.

The Mighty Roman Army

The Roman name for Britain was Britannia. At this time, the island was inhabited by native Britons belonging to many different Celtic tribes. As the Romans began their march through southeast England, one of the first tribes to fight back were the Catuvellauni. The Celtic men were fearsome warriors, but they could not stop the advance of the mighty Roman army.

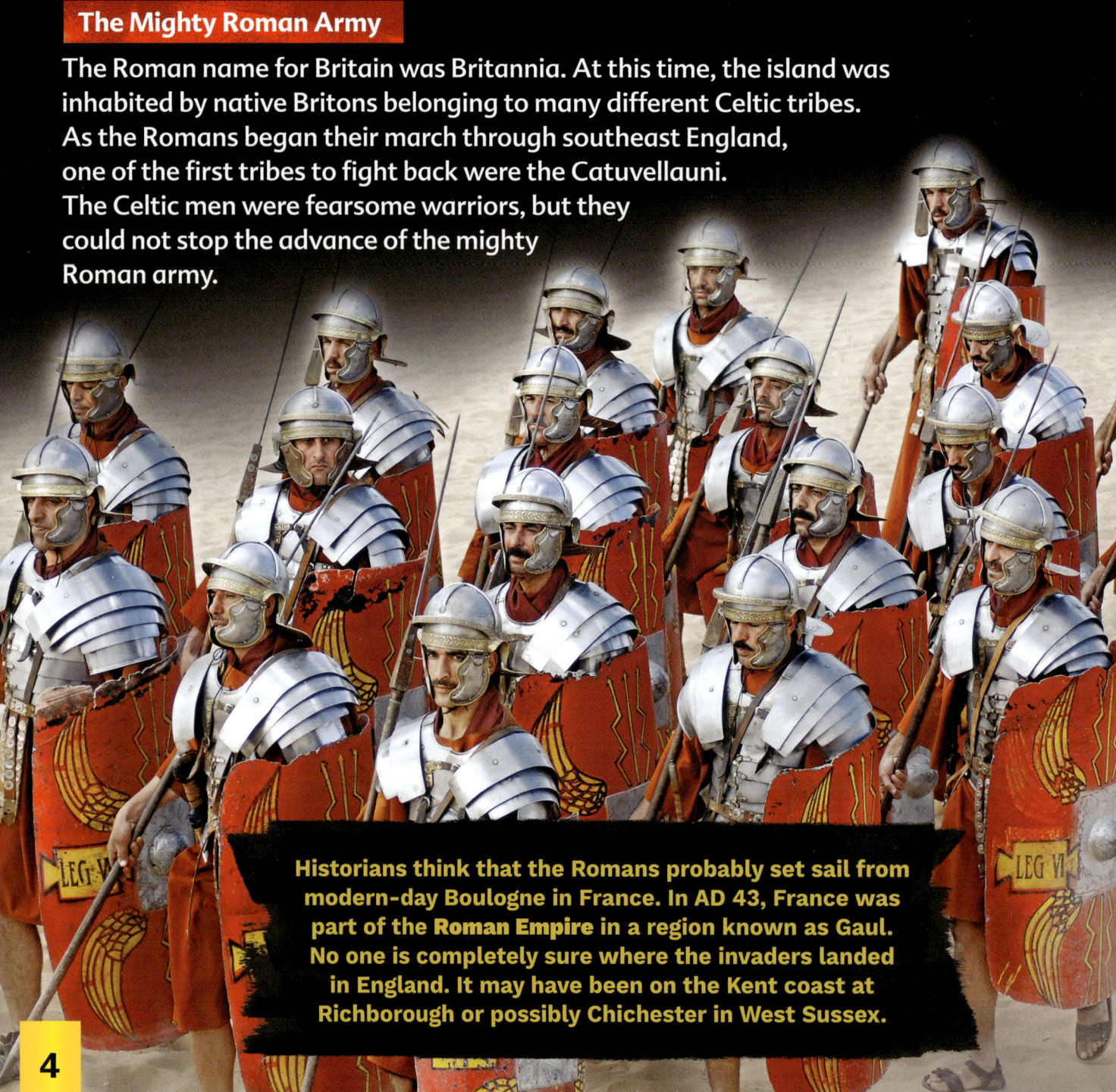

Historians think that the Romans probably set sail from modern-day Boulogne in France. In AD 43, France was part of the Roman Empire in a region known as Gaul. No one is completely sure where the invaders landed in England. It may have been on the Kent coast at Richborough or possibly Chichester in West Sussex.

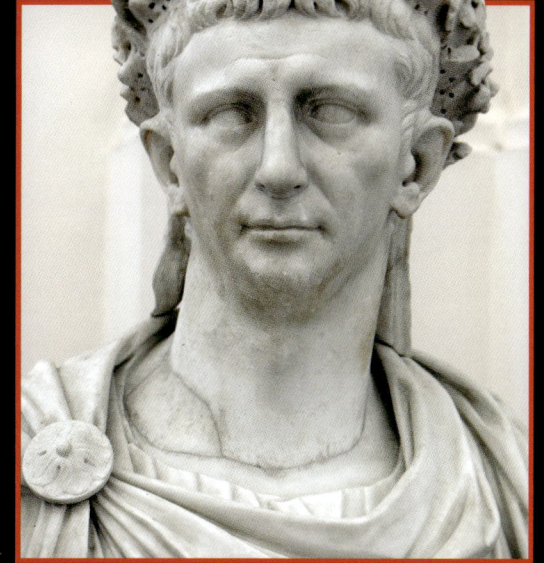

Emperor Claudius ruled Rome from AD 41 to 54.

A Triumphant Arrival

General Plautius sent a messenger to Rome to announce that the invasion was a success.

Rome's leader, the **Emperor** Claudius, came to join his troops, even bringing a war elephant with him. Triumphant, the Romans marched into Camulodunum (modern-day Colchester), the capital of the Catuvellauni people.

The Roman conquest of Britain had begun!

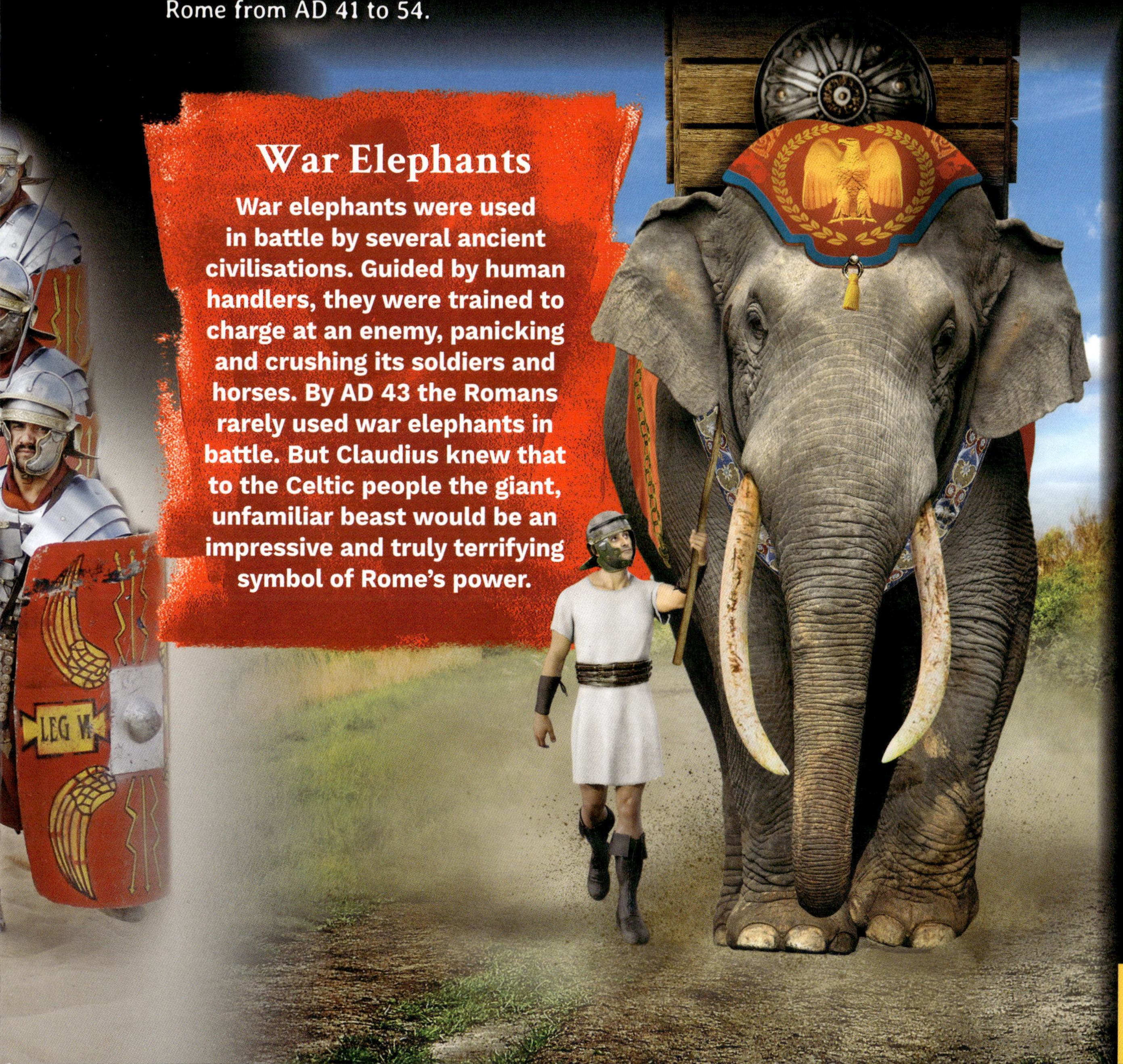

War Elephants

War elephants were used in battle by several ancient civilisations. Guided by human handlers, they were trained to charge at an enemy, panicking and crushing its soldiers and horses. By AD 43 the Romans rarely used war elephants in battle. But Claudius knew that to the Celtic people the giant, unfamiliar beast would be an impressive and truly terrifying symbol of Rome's power.

Who Were the Romans?

The ancient Romans were a powerful group of people who lived more than 2000 years ago.

Rome and the First Romans

The city of Rome was founded around the mid 700s BC. Its inhabitants were people from different tribes that lived in the region that is now modern-day Italy. They settled in Rome and became the first Romans. Over time, Rome grew in size and power. Its armies went to war with neighbouring tribes and Rome took control of the whole of Italy.

Citizens of Rome

All free men were **citizens** of Rome. Women were citizens, too, but they could not vote or become politicians. Slaves were not free, but if they were obedient and hardworking they might be able to buy their freedom or have it granted by their owners. Then they were known as a freedman or freedwoman.

Inside the home of a patrician family.

Roman Society

Roman society was chiefly made up of three main groups of people — **patricians**, **plebeians** and slaves. Patricians were the wealthy, upper-class members of society. Plebeians, or plebs, were the working class of Rome. They worked as builders, craftsmen, bakers and farmers.

Most slaves in Rome were prisoners of war. Slave dealers followed the Roman armies ready to buy captured people and defeated enemy soldiers. After one battle in Belgium in 57 BC, the Roman army took 53,000 people prisoner and sold them into slavery!

The Work of Slaves

Roman slaves worked in homes caring for children, cooking and washing clothes. Child slaves were sometimes trained as hairdressers. Patrician families often owned highly educated Greek slaves who tutored their sons in literature, history, mathematics and public speaking. Some slaves even worked as doctors.

Slaves at work

Many slaves did back-breaking work in **quarries**, cutting stone such as marble for buildings. They also worked underground in copper, lead and silver mines.

Who Ruled Rome?

• For many years after its founding, Rome was ruled by kings.

• In 509 BC, Rome became a **republic**. It no longer had one leader but was ruled by a powerful group of politicians called senators.

• Rule by the Roman Senate continued until a politician and army general named Julius Caesar decided he wanted to rule and made himself leader of Rome in 49 BC.

• Some of the senators were not happy about this new system, however, and murdered Caesar on 15 March 44 BC.

• The idea of having one great leader did not go away, however, and in 27 BC Julius Caesar's nephew and adopted son Augustus Caesar became the first emperor of Rome.

• With the rise of Augustus Caesar, the Roman Empire was born. While the Roman Senate still existed, most of the ruling power shifted to the emperor.

Augustus Caesar ruled Rome from 27 BC to AD 14.

The Roman Empire

The Romans were empire builders who wanted more than just Italy.

Empire Builders

The Romans invaded the lands of the ancient Greeks and Egyptians. They conquered parts of North Africa. They marched into many areas of Europe, including the modern-day nations of France, Spain and Germany. They headed east to modern-day Turkey, Israel and Syria. And eventually, they invaded Britain.

The Secret of Success

The main reason that Rome became so powerful was the Roman army. Highly trained and **disciplined**, Roman soldiers could march 32 kilometres in a day, swim rivers in full armour and weaponry and face enemy forces 10 times their size in battle — and win!

The remains of a Roman road in modern-day Algeria in North Africa.

It was possible to use Roman coins throughout the empire. A *denarius* from Rome could be used to buy fish in Egypt, wine in Spain, spices in Turkey or sheep in Britain!

A *denarius* with the head of Emperor Trajan

Some roads were just dirt and gravel, while others were paved with large flat stones.

Roman Rule

Sometimes, the Roman forces met resistance. But often the people they invaded did not fight back and soon became used to life under Roman rule. As long as people obeyed Roman laws and paid their taxes, they were allowed to live pretty much as they had before.

The New Romans

In time, it became possible for foreigners from conquered countries to become Roman citizens. Men from across the empire joined the army. And in AD 98, a Spanish-born general named Trajan even became Roman emperor.

Roman Roads

With hundreds of thousands of troops on the move, the Romans needed to build roads – lots of roads! It's estimated that the Roman army built more than 400,000 kilometres of roads across the empire, connecting ports, cities and military bases. Whenever possible, the roads were made long and straight, taking the shortest route from A to B.

A **mosaic** showing a Roman warship

Speaking "Roman"

The Romans spoke and wrote in Latin. In many of the places they invaded, such as Britain, few people could read and write. Once their countries became part of the empire, many people learned to read and speak the Romans' language.

Roman numerals are still used today. We see them on clocks and they often appear in names where numbers are used, such as World War II, *Jurassic Park III*, Henry VIII and Super Bowl LIII.

I	V	X	L	C	D	M
1	5	10	50	100	500	1000

A Fighting Machine

The Roman army was made up of two kinds of soldiers — legionaries and auxiliaries.

The Roman Army

Legionaries were Roman citizens. These men were Rome's **elite** fighting force. Auxiliaries were usually not citizens. These soldiers were often used to guard the **frontiers** of the empire.

Roman soldiers didn't only fight. They also built roads, bridges and fortresses, from where they could guard the territories they'd conquered.

Roman Legions

The Roman army was divided into *legions*, groups of 4000 to 6000 soldiers. A legion was then sub-divided into *cohorts* of 480 men each. And then every cohort was divided into *centuries* of 80 soldiers led by a commander known as a *centurion*.

Roman soldiers fought with *pilums*, wooden spears with sharp iron spikes. ▼

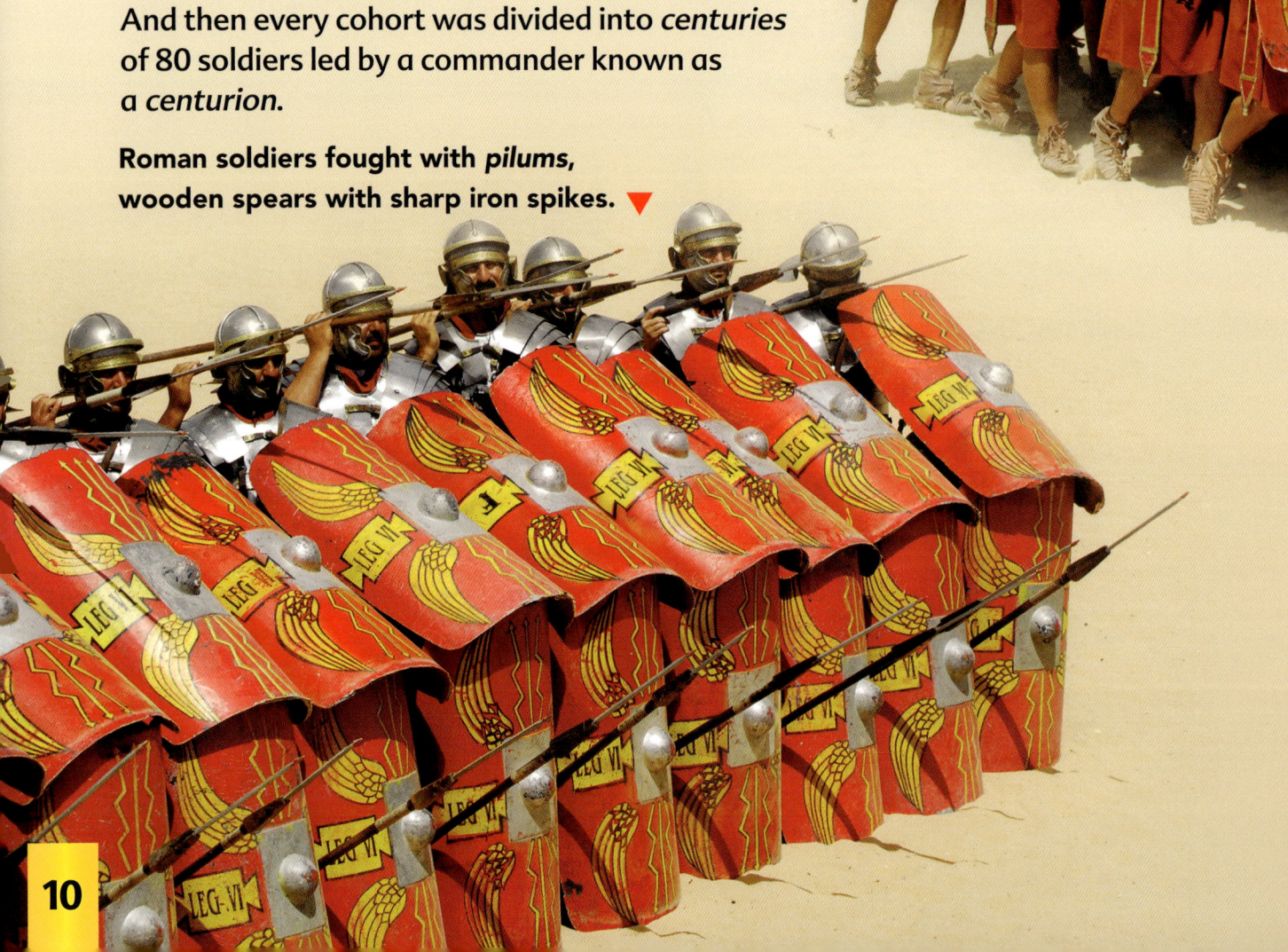

In battle, Roman soldiers marched steadily towards the enemy in a tight formation protected by their shields. At the last minute, they would unleash a hail of spears, before charging in for hand-to-hand fighting with swords. The cavalry (soldiers on horseback) would chase after enemy soldiers who tried to escape. After a battle, doctors and soldiers with medical training treated the wounded and the men dug graves and buried their dead comrades.

A re-enactment of the *testudo* formation. *Testudo* is the Latin word for "tortoise".

Making Camp

When on the march, the Roman army made camp each night. If the legions were in enemy territory, thousands of soldiers would get to work digging a wide defensive ditch around the camp's perimeter. Then cookhouses, stable areas for the horses and thousands of tents were erected. A camp big enough for several legions might cover an area the size of 80 football pitches!

A Roman soldier's armour, weapons and other kit, such as tools and cooking equipment, weighed about 35 kg.

Galea
An iron helmet that protected the back of the neck and cheeks.

Lorica segmentata
Body armour of overlapping metal plates

Scutum
A large rectangular shield curved to protect the body

Gladius
A short, light sword for close-range stabbing.

Family Life and Homes

In ancient Rome, men were in charge of the family. Women had very little independence or freedom.

A Woman's World

The life of a young woman was controlled by her father. Once she married, usually in her early teens, her husband took control, telling her what she could do and making decisions for her.

Some women had jobs, such as hairdressers or midwives. But most spent their lives cooking, making clothes, raising children and caring for the home. Wealthy women also stayed at home, spending their days managing the slaves who did their household chores.

Babies and Children

In ancient Rome, many babies died in their first year. Sometimes poor families abandoned their babies because they could not afford another mouth to feed. They left them on rubbish dumps or at a special place in the city where they might be picked up and raised as a slave. About half of all Roman children died from illness or poverty before they were 10.

Homes for the Rich

A wealthy Roman family would live in a city house called a *domus*. When the dirt, smell and noise of Rome became too much, they would visit their beautiful villa in the countryside.

Homes for Rome's Poor

The plebs, or poor workers, of Rome lived in cramped apartment blocks called *insulae*. Badly built from wood and mud bricks, the buildings often caught fire or collapsed!

Insulae had no running water or toilets. Residents collected water from nearby fountains or wells. They used public toilets, or a pot that was then emptied into the street!

A Luxurious Home

A Roman villa had a kitchen, bedrooms, toilets, a bath and even an office and library. Pictures made from mosaics covered the floors and the walls were painted with colourful **frescoes**. At the centre of the villa was the *atrium*. This beautifully decorated room had a high ceiling with an opening that allowed rainwater to fall into a pond below.

◀ This painting from the 1800s shows the atrium in a wealthy Roman home.

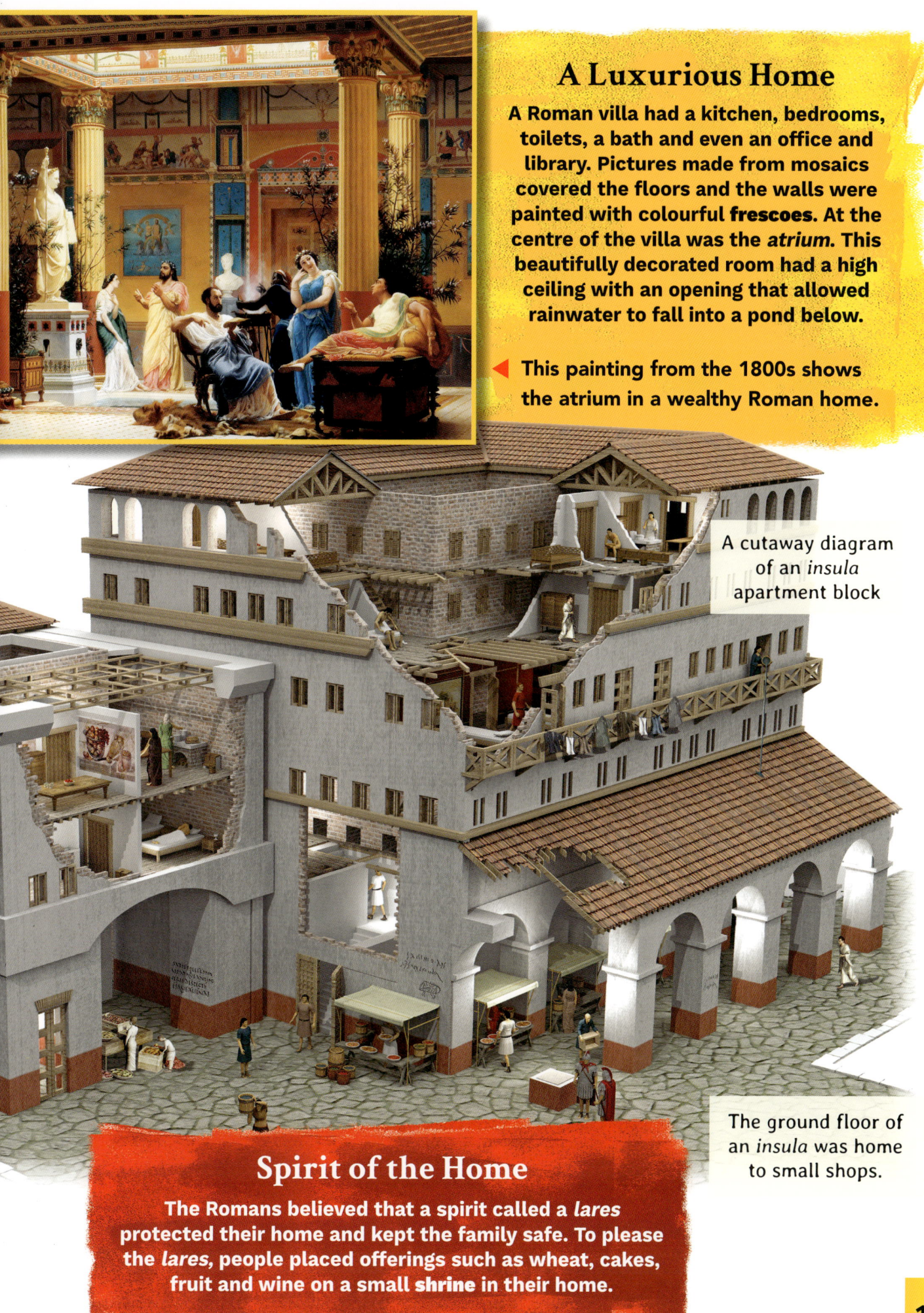

A cutaway diagram of an *insula* apartment block

The ground floor of an *insula* was home to small shops.

Spirit of the Home

The Romans believed that a spirit called a *lares* protected their home and kept the family safe. To please the *lares*, people placed offerings such as wheat, cakes, fruit and wine on a small **shrine** in their home.

Everyday Food, Take-Aways and Feasts

In ancient Rome, breakfast and lunch were small light meals. The main meal of the day was *cena*, which was eaten in the evening.

Food for the Poor

For the plebs, *cena* usually consisted of a kind of porridge made from wheat, water, salt, animal fat or olive oil and sometimes vegetables.

Food for the Wealthy

The evening meal of wealthier Romans might include bread, olives, vegetables, cheese, eggs, fish, shellfish or meat such as sausages. This was followed by fruit and cakes baked with honey, cheese, fruit, nuts, wine or spices.

Both rich and poor Romans drank white, yellow, red and black wine. Getting drunk was considered to be the behaviour of a **barbarian**. So the Romans drank their wine mixed with water.

Ancient Roman Crops

Figs

Asparagus

Wheat

Pomegranates

Courgettes

Grapes

Olives

Lentils

Peaches

Peas

An Extravagant Dinner

The wealthiest members of Roman society threw lavish feasts to impress their friends and business associates. The meal was served by slaves in a dining room called the *triclinium*.

Flamingo

Sea urchin meat

The diners lounged on couches and ate with their fingers, which they washed in perfumed water. Hosts competed to serve the most exotic foods to their guests, such as sea urchins, flamingo, ostrich, giraffe or even a dish of peacock tongues!

A terracotta *glirarium*

Air holes

Ancient Fast Food

The poor in Rome lived in tiny apartments that usually did not have kitchens. However, Rome had lots of food stalls and cafes where even the poor could afford to eat. Take-away restaurants called *thermopolia* also served cheap, ready-cooked food such as fish with bread or sausages with beans.

A Furry Snack

In Roman times people kept cute, furry dormice – but not as pets. Known as edible dormice, they were caught in the wild and then placed in pottery containers called *glirarium*. The little animals were fed on a diet of walnuts, chestnuts and acorns. Once they were fattened up, the dormice were roasted, dipped in honey and seeds and eaten as a delicious snack!

The ruins of a *thermopolium*

Counter

These holes held large jars of wine and foods, such as nuts.

Out and About in Ancient Rome

At the centre of day-to-day life in ancient Rome was the Forum.

The Forum in Rome

The Forum was a large marketplace surrounded by temples, government buildings and statues of the gods and great men from Rome's history. People came to the Forum to take part in elections, hear public speeches, watch criminal trials and celebrate religious festivals.

A Place to Meet

Romans met in the Forum to socialise with friends and do business. They also visited the many small shops and market stalls that nestled among the important buildings.

Aqueducts: Bringing Water to Rome

To bring water into Rome, engineers built 11 aqueducts. An aqueduct is a system of pipes that carries water from a source, such as a mountain spring, over many kilometres on a slight downward slope.

The Romans tunnelled through hillsides to lay the pipes for their aqueducts. And when they reached a valley or river, they built an arched bridge with a channel along its highest level through which the water could keep flowing.

Remains of the Forum in Rome

The Pont du Gard aqueduct in France

The Romans built aqueducts throughout their empire.

Ancient Roman Temples

Like all Roman cities and towns, Rome was home to many beautiful temples built to honour the Romans' many gods. Inside a temple there was a statue or carved stone image of the god to whom the temple was dedicated. Religious ceremonies took place outdoors in front of the temple. Sometimes, an animal was **sacrificed** outside on an **altar** as an offering to please the god.

The Pantheon is a Roman temple that still stands in Rome today.

Jupiter, the god of sky and thunder, was king of the Roman gods. His queen, Juno, was the goddess of marriage and childbirth.

Going Together

In ancient Rome there were many public toilets that were actually very public! As many as 20 people might "go" at the same time in a communal loo – even using it as an opportunity to chat or talk business.

A Roman public toilet

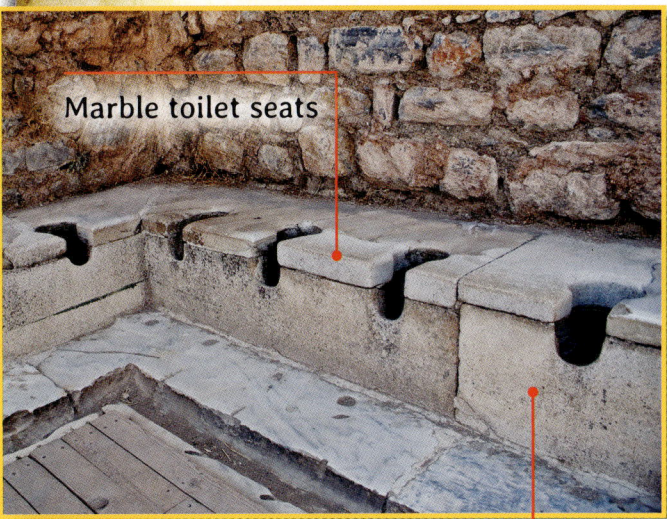
Marble toilet seats

Water ran beneath the seats carrying the waste away into underground drains.

When people had finished their business, they used a sponge on a stick called a *tersorium* to wipe themselves clean.

After using the *tersorium* you'd rinse it in a bucket of vinegar or salty water so it would be ready for the next person to use!

Roman Gladiators

In Roman times, cheering crowds packed large stadiums to watch history's most bloody and deadly sport — the gladiator games.

Why Become a Gladiator?

Most gladiators had no choice! Some were prisoners captured in wars. Others were criminals sentenced to death for serious crimes such as murder. Instead of **execution**, these men, and sometimes women, chose to become gladiators.

Gladiator School

A gladiator became the property of a manager called a *lanista*. The *lanista* owned all the gladiators at his *ludus*, or training school. A gladiator who trained in Rome would fight in the greatest arena of all — an open-air **amphitheatre** known as the Colosseum.

A *secutor* fought with a sword and shield. ▼

The word *gladiator* means "a man of the sword."

Trained to Kill

Gladiators fought to the death. Trainees had to learn how to block blows to protect their own bodies. They also learned how to do maximum damage to their opponents. A cut across a fighter's stomach could release their intestines onto the sand. A slash across the back of an opponent's knees would make it impossible for them to stand.

A *retiarius* fought with a net, dagger and three-pronged trident.

An Exciting Career!

Some gladiators actually chose this career. It was a dangerous life, but a successful gladiator could become famous – like a modern-day sportstar. By the 1st century AD, women had more freedom and many young women, especially from the upper classes, signed up to become gladiators. The excitement of life in the arena was too hard to resist!

Avoiding Death

Gladiators might go into the arena to fight just three times a year. The rest of the time they trained for hours each day. Some gladiators were very successful and lived long enough to receive the *rudis*, or wooden sword. This meant they could retire.

A Day at the Games

A day at the Colosseum was a bloody and violent treat.

Morning: Animal Fights

Wild animals, such as lions, tigers and elephants, were set loose in the arena to attack and kill each other.

Trained animal fighters called *bestiarii* also fought with the terrified creatures.

Lunchtime: Executions

Criminals who had been sentenced to death were thrown into the arena to be torn apart by the wild animals.

Afternoon: The Main Event

Two by two, pairs of gladiators entered the arena to fight. Eventually, badly injured, one fighter from each pair would fall to the ground.

The crowd shouted for mercy or for the losing gladiator's death. The emperor listened to his people and made his decision. If it was death, the winning gladiator dealt a final killer blow to his or her opponent.

The ruins of the Colosseum can still be visited today. It had many wide entrances, called *vomitoria*, to let spectators in and out.

The Colosseum covers as much ground as three football pitches and could seat more than 50,000 spectators on stone seats.

In Roman times, the arena had a wooden floor that was covered with sand to soak up the blood.

The Romans in Britain

After its successful invasion of Britain in AD 43, the Roman army marched on through southern England and into Wales.

Resistance and Peace

Some local tribes chose to fight and defy the invaders. But others made peace. In return, their leaders were allowed to live on in their kingdoms and rule them on behalf of Rome.

Villages and Towns in Roman Britain

In the 1st century AD, most Britons lived in small villages of wooden houses with thatched roofs.

When the Romans came they built towns with a forum, temples, shops and homes made of stone and bricks. They built roads, amphitheatres and large country villas.

This illustration shows the village of Silchester in England at the time of the Roman invasion.

Why Did Claudius Invade Britain?

Britain was rich in resources. It had gold, iron, copper, tin, cattle and lush farmland. But there was also another reason. Powerful people in Rome did not think of Emperor Claudius as a strong military leader. Claudius wanted to conquer Britannia to show he was worthy of being Rome's emperor.

This illustration shows the Roman town of Silchester in England, in the 300s AD.

Forum

Life in Roman Britain

Some native Britons began to enjoy the Roman way of life. Now they could go to a Roman town to sell their farm produce, visit **bath houses** and buy goods from all over the empire.

In many places, Roman settlers and the native Britons lived peacefully, even worshipping each other's gods. But peace in Britannia wouldn't last. . . .

Londinium

In the south of England, in around AD 47, the Romans built a settlement beside a great river. **Merchants** from many parts of the empire came here to trade goods and the settlement grew into a city. The Romans called their new city Londinium and it would become modern-day London.

The First Roman Invasions

Emperor Claudius wasn't the first Roman leader to invade Britain. In 55 BC (almost 90 years before Claudius's invasion), Julius Caesar landed in Kent with 20,000 Roman soldiers. However, the Roman army was met on the beaches by thousands of Celtic warriors and it was forced to retreat.

In 54 BC, Caesar tried again – this time with 50,000 soldiers. For about three months the Romans battled many tribes in southern England. But then the Roman legions were needed to control rebellious tribes in Gaul. The Romans had to withdraw from Britain once again and wouldn't return until AD 43.

Boudica's Revolt

In the east of England, the Iceni people lived peacefully under Roman rule. In about AD 60, however, their king, Prasutagus, died, unleashing a devastating chain of events.

A Brutal Betrayal

The Iceni king had left instructions that his land and wealth were to be divided — half to his daughters and half to Emperor Nero in Rome. But Prasutagus's wishes were ignored. Roman officials took everything. They attacked his daughters and brutally flogged his queen, Boudica.

A Great Army

Boudica and her people had suffered years of Roman rule and now the invaders had stolen their kingdom. The Iceni queen raised a great army of 200,000 Celtic warriors. It was time to revolt and fight back!

To look more terrifying, Celtic ▶ warriors stiffened their hair with white, chalky lime and painted their faces and bodies blue with a plant dye called woad.

Time For Revenge

Boudica and her forces stormed Camulodunum, Londinium and Verulamium (modern-day St Albans). They burned the Roman towns to the ground and massacred the inhabitants. Most of the Roman forces were fighting in Wales, but they rushed back to England to stop the revolt. Finally Boudica's army faced the hated Romans.

The Celtic warriors vastly outnumbered the Roman legions, but the superior organisation and fighting skills of the Romans won the day. At the end of the battle, it is said that 80,000 Britons lay dead and just 400 Romans.

No one knows what happened to Boudica. But a Roman historian named Tacitus wrote that the proud, warrior queen killed herself by taking poison.

A Roman historian named Cassius Dio described Boudica as "very tall", with "fierce eyes", a "harsh voice" and "a great mass of the tawniest [reddish] hair". Was his description correct? We can't say for sure. What we do know is that Dio never actually saw the Iceni queen for himself – he wasn't born until almost 100 years after Boudica's revolt!

Ancient Evidence

When **archaeologists** dig in London, they find **evidence** of Boudica's attack on Roman Londinium. About 7 metres underground there is a layer of burned brick and soil. The great battle with the Romans probably took place somewhere along a stretch of Roman road known as Watling Street. As yet, archaeologists have not discovered exactly where.

The Roman Baths

Wealthy Romans loved to have a bath every day. So they built bath houses throughout the empire.

A Sacred Spring

The city of Bath in England grew up on a spot where a naturally hot spring bubbled up from underground. The spring was a sacred place to the native Britons where they worshipped the goddess Sulis.

When the Romans came to the region, they built a bath house at the spring so they could enjoy the hot waters. They were also happy to worship the goddess of the spring, just like the local people.

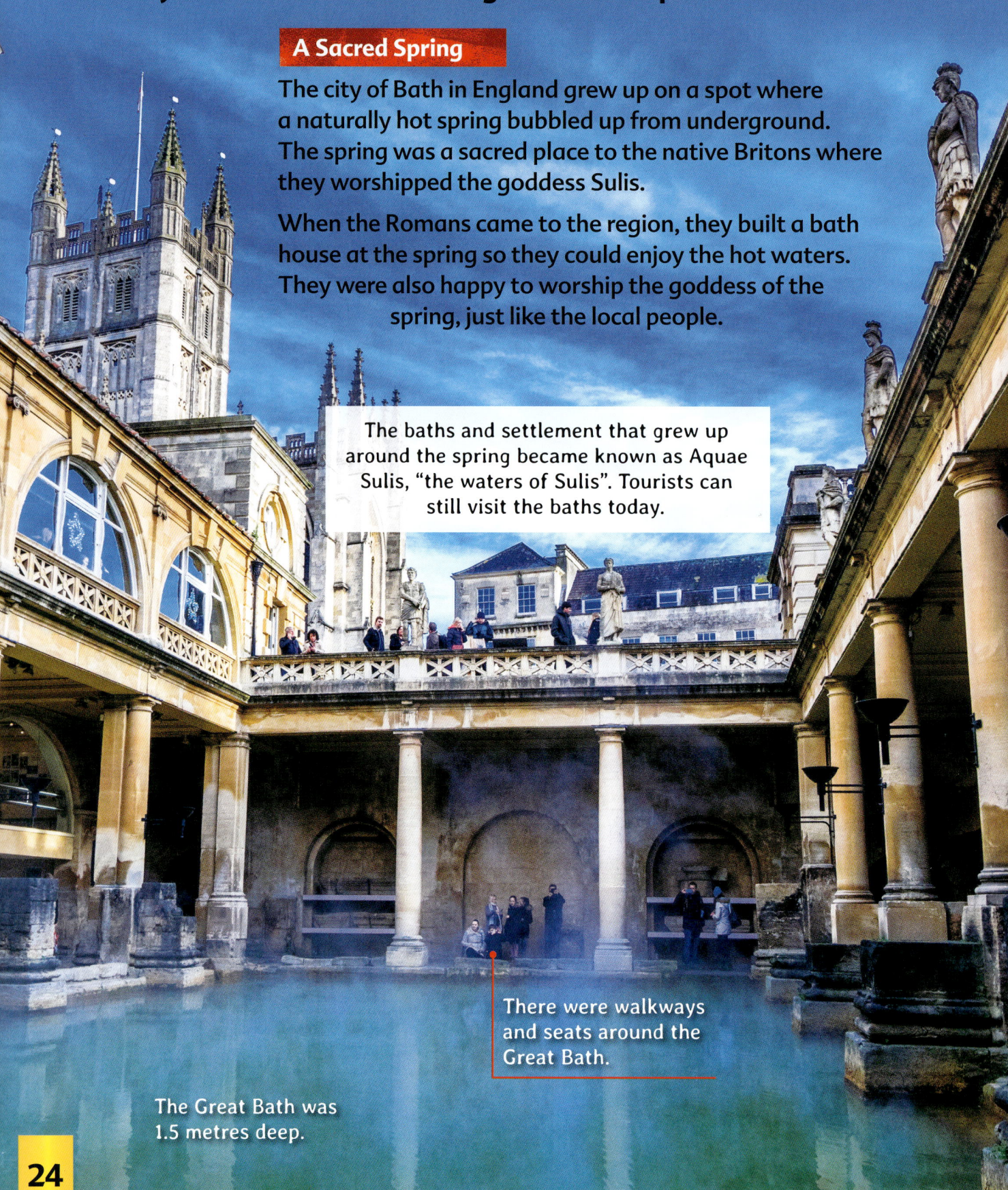

The baths and settlement that grew up around the spring became known as Aquae Sulis, "the waters of Sulis". Tourists can still visit the baths today.

There were walkways and seats around the Great Bath.

The Great Bath was 1.5 metres deep.

Healing Powers

Visitors to the baths at Aquae Sulis would get clean in the baths' steam rooms and pools. They would also spend time in the Great Bath swimming or relaxing. It was believed that the warm waters had healing powers and could make a person healthier.

Getting Clean

Both men and women visited bath houses. First they spent time in a *tepidarium* (warm steam room) followed by a visit to the *caldarium* (hot room). Next they were massaged with olive oil by a slave. Then a tool called a *strigil* was used to scrape off the oil along with dirt, sweat and dead skin. Finally, they plunged into a cold pool called a *frigidarium* to wash off the oil.

A *strigil*

A Visit to the Baths

At the baths, people did exercise, met with friends or held business meetings. They discussed politics, gambled, played board games and ate and drank. They also had beauty treatments such as manicures and having the hairs from their armpits plucked out!

A Goddess for Wishes

The Romans believed that the goddess Sulis could cure them of troubles such as constipation, skin diseases and unhappiness. At Aquae Sulis, they threw coins, jewellery and valuable objects such as silver cups into the spring to please the goddess and ask for her help.

The Romans called the goddess Sulis Minerva.

A Goddess for Curses

If a person had stolen from you or wronged you in some other way, you could scratch a curse on a small piece of lead or pewter and throw it into the sacred waters at Aquae Sulis. Then the goddess Sulis would help you by punishing the wrongdoer.

Hadrian's Wall: The Northern Frontier

By the end of the 1st century AD, most of southern Britain was under Roman control. However, the northern part of Britain, modern-day Scotland, was proving much harder to conquer!

The Wild North

The Romans called the north Caledonia. It was home to warrior tribes, many of whom refused to give in to Roman rule. Unable to conquer the north and under the constant threat of raids by the fierce northern tribes, the Roman Emperor Hadrian built a great wall to separate Roman Britain from Caledonia.

Work began on Hadrian's Wall in AD 122. It was an enormous endeavour that would take 15,000 legionaries about six years. The Roman forces also built around 15 forts for the thousands of troops that would defend the frontier. When it was complete, the wall stretched from sea to sea across northern Britain.

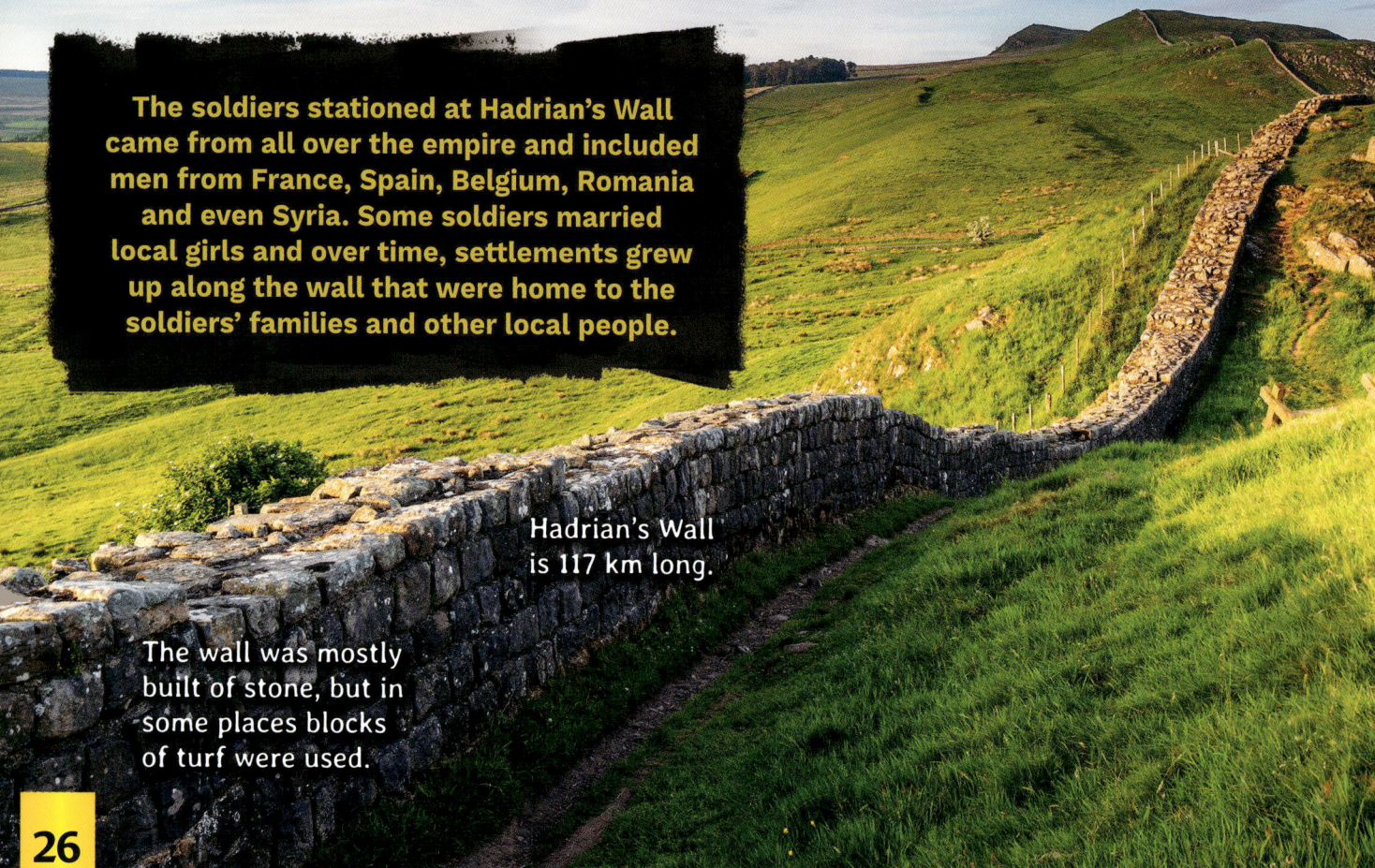

The soldiers stationed at Hadrian's Wall came from all over the empire and included men from France, Spain, Belgium, Romania and even Syria. Some soldiers married local girls and over time, settlements grew up along the wall that were home to the soldiers' families and other local people.

Hadrian's Wall is 117 km long.

The wall was mostly built of stone, but in some places blocks of turf were used.

Small, tower-like stone forts called milecastles were constructed every mile along the wall.

In Roman times the wall was about 6 metres high.

Letters from Home

Archaeologists at the Vindolanda fort at Hadrian's Wall found the remains of letters between the troops and their friends and families back home. One letter tells a soldier that the writer is sending him two pairs of sandals, two pairs of socks and two pairs of underpants!

The milecastles were also gateways where people could cross the frontier – and pay taxes!

About 30 soldiers were stationed (in barracks) at each milecastle ready to defend the wall.

The letters found at Vindolanda were written on thin, postcard-sized pieces of wood.

The End of Roman Rule

Roman rule in Britain came to an end in AD 410. Rome was under attack from tribes of nomadic people called the Visigoths. Elsewhere in the world the empire was crumbling. The Roman army had to pull out of Britain because it was needed in Italy to defend the heart of the empire.

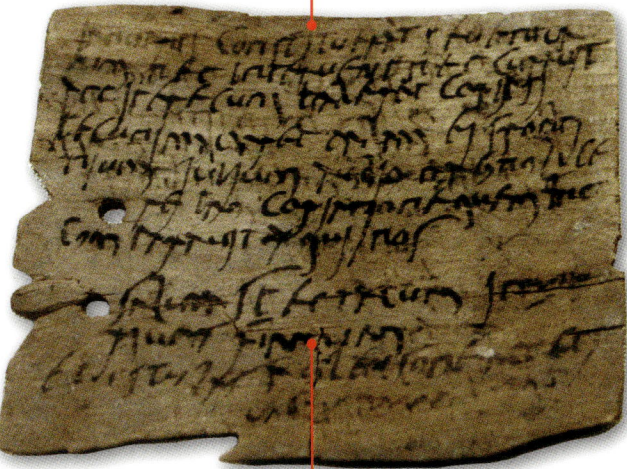

Message written in ink on one side

The address was written on the other side.

Roman Bones

Roman people from all over the empire made Britain their home.

Roman Migrants

Romans came to Britain as merchants, sailors, soldiers or slaves. Women and children travelled with husbands and fathers. And when these Roman people died in Britain, they left behind fascinating evidence about their lives and histories deep within their bones.

The First Londoners

Now an international team of scientists are studying Roman skeletons that were buried in London almost 2000 years ago. They are discovering the Romans' **ancestry**, where they were born, and even information about their diets.

Evidence from Bones and Teeth

- Ancient **DNA** (aDNA) can be extracted from a bone and from the soft, brown dentine inside a tooth. This aDNA can show a person's hair and eye colour.

- Mitochondrial DNA (mtDNA) tells scientists about a person's family stretching back many hundreds of years.

- Chemicals in food and drinking water are captured in bones, dentine and in the enamel of a person's teeth. By studying these chemicals it's possible to know what a person ate and use that information to figure out whether they were eating foods from the local area.

Scientist Rebecca Redfern examines the damaged skull of a man who may have fought as a gladiator in Roman London.

One Young Londoner

One of the Roman skeletons that have been investigated is nicknamed the Lant Street girl after the place where she was found. By studying her skeleton, DNA and chemicals in her skeleton, the young girl's story has been revealed.

• The Lant Street girl was 14 years old when she died.

• She had blue eyes.

• She was White European with White European ancestry.

• She was born in the southern Mediterranean, perhaps in an area that is now modern-day Syria, Lebanon, Egypt, Libya or Morocco.

• The Lant Street girl had been eating fish, meat and vegetables from the London area for about four to five years. This shows she came to London at the age of nine or ten.

Did the Lant Street girl travel to London with her merchant father? Perhaps she was brought to Britain as a slave or to be the bride of a Roman soldier.

Ancient and Modern Britain

The analysis of ancient skeletons has shown that Romans came to Britain from many different parts of Europe, Africa and the Middle East. In fact, just like modern-day Britain, Roman Britain was home to people from all over the world.

Glossary

altar
A large table or flat-topped block of stone used in religious ceremonies for making offerings.

amphitheatre
A circular stadium where people watched theatre performances or events such as gladiator fights.

ancestry
A person's family and ethnic history.

archaeologist
A scientist who studies the past by examining the physical remains left behind, such as buildings and skeletons.

auxiliary
A professional Roman soldier who was not a Roman citizen.

barbarian
A person who lived outside the Roman Empire who the Romans believed was violent and uncivilised.

bath house
A public building where Romans went to have baths and take exercise.

citizen
In the Roman Empire, a man or woman who was free (not a slave).

disciplined
Having a controlled way of behaving or working.

DNA
The material that carries all the information about how a living thing will look and function. DNA is short for deoxyribonucleic acid.

elite
Special with superior skills.

emperor
The leader of the Roman Empire.

evidence
Information that can be used to show that something is true.

execution
The carrying out of a death sentence.

forum
A marketplace and meeting area surrounded by temples and other buildings in a Roman town.

fresco
A mural (large painting on a wall) that was painted onto wet plaster.

frontier
The border of a country or territory.

legionary
A professional Roman soldier who was a Roman citizen.

merchant
A person (usually from history) who buys and sells goods. Merchants often travelled from place to place to do business.

mosaic
A picture or pattern made from tiny pieces of coloured glass or pottery.

patrician
A person from the upper, ruling class of ancient Rome.

plebeian
A working class person in ancient Rome. *Plebs* were citizens of Rome.

quarry
A large deep hole from which rock is dug.

republic
A country where the power is held by the people and their elected politicians, rather than a king or queen.

Roman Empire
The parts of the world that were conquered and ruled over by the Romans.

sacrifice
To kill an animal or person as part of a ritual or as an offering to a god.

shrine
A special or sacred place where a god or spirit is worshipped. A shrine might be simple — for example, a small table with candles and a statue of a god.

Index